ONCE UPON A DREAM

Yorkshire

Edited By Megan Roberts

First published in Great Britain in 2019 by:

Young Writers
Remus House
Coltsfoot Drive
Peterborough
PE2 9BF
Telephone: 01733 890066
Website: www.youngwriters.co.uk

FOREWORD

Welcome Reader, to a world of dreams.

For Young Writers' latest competition, we asked our writers to dig deep into their imagination and create a poem that paints a picture of what they dream of, whether it's a make-believe world full of wonder or their aspirations for the future.

The result is this collection of fantastic poetic verse that covers a whole host of different topics. Let your mind fly away with the fairies to explore the sweet joy of candy lands, join in with a game of fantasy football, or you may even catch a glimpse of a unicorn or another mythical creature. Beware though, because even dreamland has dark corners, so you may turn a page and walk into a nightmare!

Whereas the majority of our writers chose to stick to a free verse style, others gave themselves the challenge of other techniques such as acrostics and rhyming couplets. We also gave the writers the option to compose their ideas in a story, so watch out for those narrative pieces too!

Each piece in this collection shows the writers' dedication and imagination – we truly believe that seeing their work in print gives them a well-deserved boost of pride, and inspires them to keep writing, so we hope to see more of their work in the future!

CONTENTS

Newland St John's CE Academy, Hull

Isla-Joy Nelly Lines (8)	60
Emily Louise Conley (8)	61
Phoebe Drake-Davis (8)	62
Amy Yeomans (9)	63
Imogen Gibson (9)	64
Lois Starkey (9)	65
Jakub Andrzej Wiewiorka (9)	66
Olivia Grace Moore (7)	67
Bohan Stephenson-Smith (8)	68
Rehema Aliyii Yussuf (9)	69
Alesia Maria (8)	70
Olivia Laws (9)	71
Emilia Hayter (7)	72
Bethany Kelechi Iwuchukwu (9)	73
Millie Grace Norton (8)	74
Russell Gareth Kneller (9)	75
Dominic Peter Arnold (8)	76
Freja Tatianah Wensveen (8)	77
Evie Marie Pamela Lee (7)	78
Giuditta Nenye Ugwo (8)	79
Giulietta Nonye Ugwo (8)	80
Connor Walker (8)	81
Blake Rose (8)	82
Eliza Jane Janus (8)	83

Paull Primary School, Paull

Tyler Hartley (9)	84
Emelia Shally (9)	85
Jasmine Hornsby (9)	86
Josh Collier (8)	88
Ezmie Rose Butler (8)	89
Kai Wallace (8)	90
Scarlet Faulkner (8)	91
Drew Hicks (7)	92
Kacey Doney (9)	93
Holly Emma Witty (8)	94
Ethan Shane Gravill (9)	95
Harry York (8)	96
Lillie-Maya Bentley (8)	97
Ethan Zevan Butler (8)	98

Evie Kirkwood (8)	99
Eve Alexandra Valentine (7)	100
Ben Warrington (9)	101
Sophia Jazmine Gwynne (8)	102
Carter Grantam (8)	103

Queens Road Academy, Barnsley

Maria Tudose (10)	104
Frank Millkowski (10)	106
Hannah Rose Johnson (10)	107

Ravenfield Primary School, Ravenfield

Lola Frances Sanderson (10)	108
Romanie Alice Easthope (10)	109
Alex Watson (10)	110

Saltburn Primary School, Saltburn-By-The-Sea

George Sainsbury (8)	111
Eddie Dolphin (8)	112
Alex Grant (8)	113
Henry James Robinson (8)	114
Alfie Robert Gregory (8)	115
Ellie Cochrane (7)	116
Evie Marie Preston (7)	117
Samuel Robson (8)	118
Ollie Dolphin (8)	119
Izak Rees (8)	120
Talay Dechbamrung (8)	121
Jacob Williamson (7)	122
Oscar William Gill (8)	123
Lorraine Crown (8)	124

Southroyd Primary School, Pudsey

Hana Qaisar (9)	125
Harry Fletcher (8)	126

Sunnyfields Primary School, Scawthorpe

The Parks Academy, Orchard Park Estate

Townfield Primary School, Doncaster

West Road Primary School, Moorends

THE POEMS

How I Feel

S adness cries to me
A dark feeling creeps me out
D ark power can come to you
N either of your friends wants to play
E ven though you are sad, you smile
S ad people are alone
S hamed people feel troubled

H opefully, I get home safely
O n a night, I pray for luck
P ainful things make me hope
E verything is something, something to hope for

H appily, I go outside to play
A pples make me happy and healthy
P eople make me laugh
P eople make me smile
Y esterday was the best day ever.

Sadiyah Ayub (9)
Bradford Academy, Bradford

Ghost Cube

A golden star shoots towards me
It stops and hovers in slow motion around me
I touch it out of curiosity
It transforms into a monstrosity
A mystic, monstrous cube appears
My brain is filled with fear
I enter the cube, fearful, and find
A friendly, cheerful cyborg
He leads me to an abandoned, haunted house
Crawling with spiders and a mouse
"I have been waiting for your help
To transform my brother Kelp," the cyborg yelped
Just then Kelp walked down the stairs
Acting like he didn't care
"This house is mine and I don't share!"
Yelled kelp as he threw us down the cellar stairs
I glanced up and I am filled with fright
Dust! Spiders! Cobwebs!
What a sight
The friendly cyborg yelped,
"The button! The button! That'll stop Kelp!"
"What button?" I asked
"In this cellar, a button lies
If you push it my brother Kelp survives."

Under the stairs, I see a light
What a delight!
Pushing the button, I feel relieved
Waiting to see what has been achieved
The cellar door opens with a crack
Kelp enters with a shriek
"What have you done?" he screams
"Something that cannot be undone,"
The cyborg replied
Suddenly, there is a long silence
Before Kelp gives up his defiance
"Brother," whispers Kelp
"The virus is deleted!" the cyborg yelps
"Thank you," echoes around my head
Suddenly, I find myself in bed
The sunlight beaming through the curtains
I wonder if it was a dream for certain.

Rajab Suleman (7)
Bradford Academy, Bradford

Once Upon A Dream I Am Lost

In my dream, I am lost
I need to find my parents, but at what cost?

The weather is foggy and there is no one to be seen
Then in the distance I can see a man but he looks mean

As the man approaches me
He shouts out my name and invites me to tea

I then find myself in a strange house
And sitting opposite of me is a very large mouse

The mouse looks scary with very sharp teeth
I then feel his hands grab my legs from underneath

I am now trying to run, but I cannot
Someone, please help me, I'm in an awkward spot

Then through the door comes my dad
He is dressed as a superhero and looks mad

Dad punches the mouse in his head
And the wicked mouse and the man are now dead

I felt relieved and happy
That Dad saved me from this awful chappy

I then wake up in my bed
It was a dream all in my head.

Zain Alam (8)
Bradford Academy, Bradford

My Best Dream

While I was sleeping, I had a dream
I went to a tennis competition
I was excited, I was on my friend's team
Which I was happy about
So I was kind of scared
Because there were people who are way better than me
It was my turn, I got the person who I was playing against with
So my friends went up next and she got out, I was sad for her
So I thought after I finish the competition
I would give a gift to her
Then it was the last round
If I win this, I will come first place
So I went to play and got him out and I won
I was very happy, this was the best dream I'd ever had.

Oliwia Oska (9)
Bradford Academy, Bradford

Mr Clown

Hello Mr Clown
I think I heard you this morning
I swam to find your phone
And it gave me quite a shock

Dark brown socks and my colourful hair
Can be seen through the building
And, when I see your shoes with no colour, as straight
as a piece of paper
My brain still remembers everything

Let me hover on your hard head
Take me to the sun
I can feel the sun on my cheeks
Waiting for me on the grass

The sun is setting, you must go by
I can feel the waves of the sea
And then, in the sea, I can see your face
Tomorrow, I know you will sleep well.

Theo Brogden (9)
Bradford Academy, Bradford

Lunch With The Royals

Oh, dear Queen
I couldn't find your jewels
But I did find your palace rules
Looking here, looking there, looking everywhere
But the jewels were found nowhere

Tut, tut, tut
Is it Princess Charlotte?
Her big, round eyes
Leave you mesmerised

As I toss and turn throughout the night
I started to wonder, under the moonlight
Are they hidden in a place no one can reach?
In the kiddie kingdom where the queen would never believe?

As the sun awakens
I see you fading
I look back and see a mist of fog
Oh, now I'm going to miss you till night.

Eshal Saleem (8)
Bradford Academy, Bradford

My Dreams

I've dreamt of a land of sweets
I've dreamt of a land of chocolates
I've dreamt of a land of wishes
And a land of wells
I've dreamt of a land with no shouting teachers and no
lessons
I've dreamt of getting my A-plus scores up
And doing fun stuff with my teachers and my friends
I've dreamt of my teacher never getting extremely mad
with us ever again
I've dreamt of what kind of person I'll be when I'm
older
I've dreamt of what kind of loving, loyal friend and
teammate.

Randisia Dyett (10)
Bradford Academy, Bradford

Athletes

A mazing and strong, always giving it their all

T errific, always trying to win and always being confident

H igh-powered and healthy, working hard

L egit and powerful, being positive at competitions, empowered

E very day they train and are competitive

T alented and ready to win, flexible and mighty

E nergetic, muscular, the best way to be

S wiftly they go on beams and bars and they started the show.

Kianna Ava Lees (9)
Bradford Academy, Bradford

Mythical Tale

Fairies and unicorns, mythical creatures
Trying to find my home, but isn't to be seen

I wonder who can help me
I wonder who can hear me
I hope that someone helps me
Before it gets scary

Look! Some fairies and even some unicorns
I really hope they'll help me, even a monster will do!
Help, Unicorn! Yaa!
Thank you Unicorn, come on darling
Let's take you to the wizard
And take you home.

Sukeena Sherazi
Bradford Academy, Bradford

Magical Doll Pixies!

P icture perfect, I have something to tell you
I got a new giant doll and I wanted to show you
X' s and the roll finishes, here it is
I love it, but look, she has wings, she might fly
E xtreme, she actually might be
S uddenly, the doll flies and looks so beautiful.

Fatimah Al Zubaedi (8)
Bradford Academy, Bradford

Dream Land

In my dream, you can see
Unicorns, dragons, fairies and me
You can follow a path by a bee
To a castle opened with a golden key
There are mermaids that you can see
Swimming in the shimmering sea
And, there's me having afternoon tea
With a dragon called Dee.

Holly Leetham (9)
Bradford Academy, Bradford

Matrix

M an who fights robots
A nd moves between different worlds
T ry to save people
R ing for a little help
I mpossible is nothing, written by
X avi!

Xavier Okwieka (7)
Bradford Academy, Bradford

Once Upon A Dream

Once upon a dream
I can see a real heart and machines and other
surgeons helping me
I realised I'm with ill and poorly people and other
surgeons
I'm in a theatre room in a hospital
I start to feel under pressure and nausea but happy
Because I was helping people

When I was at the hospital
My friend told me your heart pumps as hard as a
tennis ball
So squeeze a tennis ball until it has a dent in it
That's how hard your heart pumps
When you are a surgeon, you can hear different noises
like *beep, beep*
Or surgeons communicating

When you're in a hospital
The bed runs around and it is as hard as a rock
At the same time, I want to help people

Fatima Bareerah (8)
Lane End Primary School, Leeds

My Future As A School Teacher

Once upon a dream
Where I was a school teacher
I'd greet the pupils one by one
And say, "It's nice you meet you."

I'd teach them English and maths too
On Wednesday, I'd teach PE
The children were as giddy
As people at a party
When I tell them we're doing IT

I'd help them read and help them write
I'd lend them a book to read at night

The children go *bang*
The children are happy
When they're in the playground
They sometimes get snappy

But before they go home at the end of the day
We will recap the work we've done and I will say,
"Your work is amazing
Now go home and share it with Mum."

Layla-Grace Amanda Tansey (8)
Lane End Primary School, Leeds

Sing Until I Win

Once upon a dream
I was a singer auditioning with my song
The competition has begun
Then the yellow microphone goes *squeak*

It's Team Red's turn, their singing
Is as beautiful as a newborn baby
Team Red is also known as the Hot Volcanoes
They sang, 'What Do You Mean'.

It's my turn now, I remembered all my training
When I walked in, I saw lots of fans
I sang, 'Once I Was Seven Years Old.'

One day later, I found out that I won
I was overjoyed
So I collected my trophy
The trophy was as shiny as a star in the sky

I walked out of the stadium
It was night-time
All I see is the stadium
A funfair and Big Ben.

Lucas Vinter (8)
Lane End Primary School, Leeds

The Magical Dream

My dream is to go to Enchantia
When I'm there, I see rainbows
As colourful as chameleons
My dream is to see unicorns
As beautiful as a Disney princess
The waterfalls giggled as they poured down
The unicorn landed with a boom!

When I walked further, I could see
The sun always smiling at me
After that, the flowers danced
By nodding their heads
Isn't that cute? Above my head
I can see butterflies giggling

There are lots of friendly animals in Enchantia
There are dancing ladybirds
Talking puppies and singing flowers
In the evening, I lie on the grass
Near the singing flowers
And I watch the sky
Mixing colours walking in the sky.

Testimony Abejoye (8)
Lane End Primary School, Leeds

The Magical Unicorn

I had a dream
I am in a sweet unicorn world
And the people are made out of scrumptious, yummy
chocolate
I can see unicorns everywhere, it is beyond magical
I can see bubblegum clouds in the dead of night
I can see a unicorn flying like a cheetah

I am with a unicorn
She is as light as a feather
She is wondrous, wonderful
My unicorn is as light as the wind
My unicorn is a magical creature

My heart is beating like a racing car
My body is heavy like a large stone
I felt a shake when the wind whistled
I felt a shake when I woke up on a bubblegum cloud
But sadly, my unicorn flew back to her magical home.

Mahek-Zahra Batool (8)
Lane End Primary School, Leeds

My True Destiny

Once upon a dream
I went to work and sat down
But when I started painting
I heard a twinkle
But I didn't know what it was so I carried on painting
But, when I had finished, it rose from my bare hands
Then I saw it come to life

Her hair was as pink as a butterfly
Her face was as white as snow
But there was something missing, it was her tail!
She told me that someone had stolen it
And hidden it in the human world

After a hundred years
I found it and I knew
My true destiny was to be a hero.

Amelia Rose Barton (8)
Lane End Primary School, Leeds

20

The King Of The Ocean

Once upon a dream, I was the ocean
And I treated every sea animal
And water dragons as a pet
I became the king of the ocean
Because the king died

Then someone hypnotised the queen
And someone else who looked like a mermaid
Became queen

When the sun came down
Every sea animal slept
And my castle sits on the sand
That's underwater

My castle has a huge pearl for a door
Gold for the colour and seaweed for the carpet
Whenever someone knocks on my door
It will go *ding!*

Urfan Khesrawi (8)
Lane End Primary School, Leeds

My Future Life

Once upon a dream
I went to see Leeds versus Liverpool
I saw a football stadium and
My friend and footballers
I am with a famous footballer and
I was at a football stadium with my uncle
I was thrilled, wow!

When I grew up, I was in the same team as my friends
When I scored a goal
The crowd shouted as loud as a lion's roar
When we drew with the other team
We had to go to penalties
Whoever scored five goals
They would win the semi-finals
And we won!

Samuel Gomes (8)
Lane End Primary School, Leeds

This Is My Dream

One morning, I went to school
The children were screaming as loud as a jungle
I hit the table with a bang!
Then everyone began working silently

I am working on my computer
My keyboard groans as I press the keys
My mouse giggles as I move it around
My computer gets tired as I use all of its energy

Now I'm printing something
I inserted the paper as fast as a rocket
I turned on the printer and it ate the paper
It's now raining ink in the printer.

Zaryaab Keyan (8)
Lane End Primary School, Leeds

Ministry Walk

Once upon a dream
I was getting into bed
Suddenly I found myself in the Forbidden Forest
My dog was still snoring away
She woke up and howled
We set off and suddenly, we fell down a hole
We went past Diagon Alley
Then a bright light came upon our eyes
It was as bright as a firefly
Then I saw Rubeus Hagrid and Albus Dumbledore
They took me around the vault
And as quick as a rocket
Rubeus disappeared
Then, I found it was a dream
And I was in my bed.

Jack Harry Johnson (8)
Lane End Primary School, Leeds

The Hospital Goes Slow

Once upon a dream
The hospital was running slow
But there were sick patients
The sun was cooking the hospital

The hospital was fresh, had a lovely breeze
The patients are ill, I ask what happened to them
But it was a big surprise, they were pretending that
they were ill
I said, "What is this for?" I laughed, "Hahaha!"

I said, "Are you joking?" They said no
I closed my eyes
I was shocked about this.

Angel Daudi (8)
Lane End Primary School, Leeds

My Dream To The Moon

I have a dream and my dream is to fly to the moon
I woke up the next morning
And found myself in space with wings
My wings danced while I sang along
It was like a dream come true

As I flew, I saw Earth spin around
I saw the sun burning like the oven
It was like a dream
All of a sudden someone tapped me
I turned around and saw a fairy
I danced with her and my wings sang
But then my wings took me and the fairy home.

Hiyab Bereket Weldemikael (8)
Lane End Primary School, Leeds

Football Daydream

A football appeared
From the playground
And I nervously kicked it

The ball whooshed around the net
And bounced out
I saw brilliant players
I was with my dad

If this match didn't happen
Nothing would've turned the ball
Into a mysterious, magical one
And the ball is as shiny as the sun

If this day came up
Everybody would scream
It was Spurs vs Man City
Man City lost to Spurs.

Mamado Sello Ly (7)
Lane End Primary School, Leeds

Kasiius' Poem

When the dragons race, they are like lightning
And when they eat their meat, it's redder than fire
And the skeletons are whiter than marshmallows

The dragon's claws are sharper than a knife
The dragons can see the magic
The dragons are in the sky, then ninjas

And then the dragons see the volcano erupting
And then they turn into gods.

Kasiius Richardson (8)
Lane End Primary School, Leeds

My Superhero Life

Once upon a dream
I was a Transformer girl
It was so fun
I saved a hundred people at least
I jumped and flew
I turned into anything I wanted
I turned into a cat, a dog, anything I wanted

I turned into a cat with ginger fur and white and black
colours
As a cat, I saved people from a hundred-foot drop
They were frightened.

Ruby-Jane Hall (8)
Lane End Primary School, Leeds

Cops And Police

My dream is to be a cop
To be as fast as a cheetah in the car
I can see people driving a car and going to shops

The car is screaming like a baby asking for food
The gun shot the target with a bang and boom!
I can see tall skyscrapers and people walking about

I hope one day I'm a real policeman
And can save everyone.

Rayyan Maalik (8)
Lane End Primary School, Leeds

Roller Skater Valley

Once upon a dream
I went outside and saw trees
And beautiful bluebirds
As blue as a diamond

I was with Miss Nelson and fell
And realised we were in Roller Skate World
And I was cheerful

The roller skates grabbed onto our feet
We skated down the hill
The path was grey like a raincloud
And black like tarmac.

Jade Janssens (8)
Lane End Primary School, Leeds

Football Forever

Once upon a dream
Thousands of fans and football players
Were making lots of noise

The ball curved
And swiftly hit the back of the net
With a huge bang from the roof

The ball flew over the crossbar by an inch
The fans were excited
But then the ball missed
And the fans sat down.

Kenzie Lee Booth (8)
Lane End Primary School, Leeds

The Dream Of The Ocean

I had a nightmare
My nightmare is about a megalodon

A megalodon is as big as a giant
I can see the wind giggling
As it flew in the air

I had a nightmare
The ocean cried
As the megalodon swam through the water
I can see the coral crying
Because the megalodon sat on the coral.

Sienna Rose Crossley (7)
Lane End Primary School, Leeds

Shay's Poem

I can see space
Where the really bright moon is
Where the stars shine like glitter
The rocket whizzed back to the moon
I am in a rocket too
I go flying to the moon
Like a boomerang
The moon is kind
When I land with a boom
I step out...

Shay Hunter (7)
Lane End Primary School, Leeds

The Dream World

It's very dark in space
My tiger is as big as an elephant
And the moon is covered in dust
Stars shine on your face
And you can hear the whooshes
From the rocketship
You can see Jupiter.

Hekma Fuseini (8)
Lane End Primary School, Leeds

To Be A Firefighter

My truck is as big as a skyscraper
And my helmet is as red as a fire
My hose splashes out water
As cold as Antarctica

If the fire roars
I will put it out
With my water as cold as Antarctica.

David Milnes (8)
Lane End Primary School, Leeds

The Artist Land

I have a dream
My paintbrush is as big as a pencil
My paper screamed like a child
My beautiful painting crashed on the ground with a
boom!

I have a dream
I can see a paintbrush dancing.

Annabelle May Barton (8)
Lane End Primary School, Leeds

This Is My Dream

I am in a beautiful and magnificent candy world
I can see some chocolate bunnies
I can see a candy castle and
It is as colourful as a rainbow.

Steven Jackson (8)
Lane End Primary School, Leeds

My Dragon And Unicorn

My dragon and unicorn are my favourites
We've always been good friends
And things are about to take a turn for the worst
Because they're from opposite ends
They have been summoned to fight on a battlefield
Where both families must actually fight
And all I can do is watch from afar
To find out who is actually right
"The winner will rule the kingdom," said a man
As everyone begins to prepare
But all I see are tears in their eyes
As Dragon and Unicorn stare
All of a sudden, as the first swords collide with a *cling*
There's a flash and amazing thunder hits
I awaken and find myself in a doze
"Was it a dream?" I asked myself and wondered
I poked my head out from under my sheets
Hoping to get an answer from my epic dream and more
But as I look up, I find myself in a unicorn and dragon battlefield of war
Now my unicorn and dragon are friends
We can live happily again.

Amaara Bukhari (9)
Madni Academy, Savile Town

The Dream Of A Young Girl

I had a dream about unicorns and fairies
They live in a palace in the clouds
I had a dream about this
I entered the clouds and saw their palace
It was colourful and amazing
I was shocked because I saw the unicorns and the
fairies
I went closer to them and said hi
The fairies were really glittery
And the unicorns were colourful
They said hi back to me, the unicorn was talking
I said to myself, "I never knew unicorns could talk."
There were rainbow water fountains
They asked me if I wanted to be their friend
So I said yes, the fairies made me one of them
She made me a fairy, she showed me around
When I got used to the palace, I started to live there
I made lots of friends
We lived happily ever after.

Maryam Imran (8)
Madni Academy, Savile Town

Teacher

I am a pretty teacher
Wearing a flowery dress
A pen in my hair and book under my arm
Pupils not paying attention
So I have to be strict with them
The class in the forest and we are on a camping trip
Excited and fresh in the forest
Learning to do modelling
And walking and a game of hide-and-seek
I dream about teaching
Furniture, table, and chairs from bamboo sticks
I see myself like a good, strong teacher.

Saarah Amin (7)
Madni Academy, Savile Town

Mr Footballer!

Mr Footballer, Mr Footballer,
I could see you last night
I saw you fighting through mean clouds
To find your football boots!
You gave me quite a fright

Your bright orange and red football boots
Could be seen from far and wide
And when I see your football boots
It makes me forget everything.

Let me get in your football clothes
And pretend I am a footballer
With your boots on me.

The time is running out
I should get going
I forgot to say goodbye.
It will be boring without you
I hope to see your boots shining in the clouds when
you're gone.

Declan Greenwood (9)
Middlestown Primary Academy, Middlestown

A Bear On A Shelf

Once there was a bear on a shelf
A fluffy, cute one but no one could get
Unless they had two hundred pounds
Everyone wanted it but their mums said no!
But they sneaked it in the trolly and their mums didn't
know
So they took it home and no one knows
So now they love it and off it goes.

Isabelle Louise Proctor (8)
Middlestown Primary Academy, Middlestown

Manuela

Many children in my class don't like me as a friend
But a real friend is one person
That you trust and believe and plays with you

A child in my class always does bad things to me
But I don't, won't tell the teacher because, if I do
The teacher is gonna talk to the child
And then the child will never talk to me again
And how am I going to make friends?

None of the children in my class were helping me with anything
And, when I ask them for help they will say,
"I forgot the answers," or "Ask her, she knows the answer,"
Or the more useful, "I don't know!"

Unfortunately, I don't have one friend yet
But I will try my best to have one
Excited to feel the happiness of having one friend

Later, after I found out how to make friends
I said to myself, "I will make sure that I will have one friend."

And, finally the end of my poem
I think that this will teach you that, if you don't have
one friend yet
Wait and you will get one good one.

Manuela Yeboah (9)
Newington Academy, Hull

Wonders Of Space

One time, I sat on a chair
In front of a microscope
I took a deep glare
What's that I could see?
Not a nightmare, in fact, a blue sea
Let me take another look around
Ha! Silly me! Silvery moon
I see your face, high in the sky
That is your place
That dark light that we all know
Colour opposite from snow
Up in the sky, I admired a beautiful sight
Of a planet called Saturn, in the night
On a dark winter night, I saw
The stars shining bright
Your symmetrical shape
Your natural light
Well, that's all for today
I'll come back another day.

Daniel Grzona (10)
Newington Academy, Hull

Dog's Wish

I wish of a dog which is fun and crazy like a frog
When I come back from school, he will be so happy
To lick my chin to my skull
When I go for a walk with my dog, he will chase the
ball
Like a thunderbolt
When I go training, he'll not be allowed to go on the
pitch
But instead, I will take him to the beach
When we will come back from the walk
We will sit and watch TV
My dog will be my best friend forever and ever
Because he will follow me wherever
My wish and moaning is a goal to dog owning.

Nataniel Zoch (10)
Newington Academy, Hull

Lightning Man

S peeding across the sky, faster than a plane
U nique abilities, Lightning Man's the name
P owered by electricity, I just can't be stopped
E very evil enemy getting dropped!
R ight around the universe, people know my name
H elping the defenceless, that's this hero's game
E ndless cool adventures, daring deeds I do!
R ed and blue lasers shooting from the ceiling
O pen up my eyes, realising I was dreaming.

Lenny Jones (10)
Newington Academy, Hull

I Have Superpowers!

S uddenly, we arrive at the bank

U nderstanding where to make a deposit

P olice start to appear

E verybody is scared

R unning springs to mind

P owers! I forgot I have powers!

O n my powers came

W here my muscles grow in a fight

E veryone stands aside

R obbery in progress

S isters and brothers work together and help stop the bad guys.

Luca McCall Baker (10)
Newington Academy, Hull

Scary Sounds Of Monsters

M oaning I heard the crack of fresh bones

O h no! I think it could be a monster!

N obody was prepared for this battle

S o then I got a metal, stiff sword

T hen I have to go and see and open the door

E xcitingly I came and then the monster came

R unning like a panther, I went to my bed

S uddenly, I woke up and heard roars again.

Alan Drewno (10)
Newington Academy, Hull

The Stars

In the night
Shining bright
They all sleep tight
Up high, in the sky
They all seem very shy
By their side
Is the moonlight
They take us on a ride
Worldwide
Brave and pride
Overnight

S hining bright across the sky
T hey all seem very shy
A round and around the sky, we see them
R ight before bed is the best time to greet them
S tars, oh stars, more beautiful than a gem.

Lena Andrejeva (10)
Newington Academy, Hull

Candy Land

D reams can be about anything, even candy

R unning around in Candy Land is hard because it is very sandy

E verything is tasty, it's all made of sweets

A ll nice and sugary, lots and lots of treats

M y family is with me too, they are happy to eat some goodies

S ometimes in Candy Land, it can be cold, so make sure you bring your hoodies.

Ben Leeman (10)
Newington Academy, Hull

The Dream Of Animals

I had a dream about a dog
Playing around in the fog
He found a unicorn sat on a log
Then my kitten ripped my mitten
Oh, what a silly kitten
The kitten chased the fox
That fell out of a box
The fox's name is Rox
And he has smelly socks
The fox ran away
Because the kitten wanted to play
This was my dream
And I didn't scream.

Savanna Thompson (9)
Newington Academy, Hull

Footballer

One sunny day, when I was at the football stadium
with my family
And friends we saw Mo Salah go to score
He got it in the top corner
I was happy because he was on the team me and my
friends liked
But it came with a great bang!
Liverpool was winning as Mo Salah got them two goals
in a row!

Charlie Wilkinson (10)
Newington Academy, Hull

Fairies

F airies are mystical creatures
A re like mini angels
I have my own special fairy
R ecognisable by their sparkles of light
I t is very rare if you see one
E ve is my fairy's name
S he is older than time.

Alexa Simpson (10)
Newington Academy, Hull

Sweet Dreams

Sweet dreams are amazing
When you wake up you feel amazing and happy
If it isn't a nightmare

S leep
W ondering
E ndless
E verlasting
T ragic

D reaming
R efreshed
E xploring
A mazing
M agnificent.

Amber Rose Scaum (10)
Newington Academy, Hull

Getting Lost

I couldn't see a thing last night
I walked through the foggy forest
And it gave me the chills
The forest's darkest leaves are pouring down
It cannot be seen from a mile
And when I find people I feel happy
We can survive until the end.

Dzhelil Shaban (9)
Newington Academy, Hull

Dreams

D reams come true

R eally experiencing it

E xplaining your thoughts

A vailable to anyone

M ake sure you believe in it

S ome of it is in your heart for all your life.

Konrad Zawierucha (9)
Newington Academy, Hull

My Bad Dream

D arkness in a hole

R eal? Is this real?

E ek! Was that a monster?

A m I still on Earth?

M ore questions running in my head

S uddenly, I wake up, oh it was a dream!

Oliwia Styga (10)
Newington Academy, Hull

Unicorn Dreams

U nicorns live in enchanted forests
N ever seen by humans no matter how hard we seek
I close my eyes and sometimes they pop into my head
C ome quick! A unicorn appeared on a pink, fluffy cloud
O n its back I climb and hold on tight
R iding in an enchanted forest, as fast as a cheetah
N ight-time whispers and fills the air with dreams

D aring leaps and squeals of joy
R ound the rainbow trees, the horn leads the way
E ach horn is unique, special and rare
A unicorn has sparkles in its hair
M agic, mystical adventures begin
S o now do you believe in unicorns?

Isla-Joy Nelly Lines (8)
Newland St John's CE Academy, Hull

Unicorns Are Real

U nder the trees
N earby, the girls are
I n total fear because they are lost
C lumping loudly through the forest
O ver the mountains came a unicorn
R ight beside them, the unicorn stopped to help
N ow they knew the unicorn was friendly
S uddenly, she flew them home

A ll the girls were so happy
R ight then, they wanted her to stay
E smay and Emily especially wanted this

R eally unicorns are real
E mily's family was so happy
A ll the people wanted to see the unicorn
L ovely family lived forever, happily ever after.

Emily Louise Conley (8)
Newland St John's CE Academy, Hull

My Enchanted Dream

U nder the night sky

N icely, I can dream

I can see some sort of horn

C arefully, I see something fluttering

O n my bed, there is a little fairy

R ight next to me, there is a unicorn

N ight is now turning enchanted

S omehow in the sky, there is a dragon

F lying in the sky, it is like a red star flying

A round, it's awesome. Am

I dreaming?

R eally, this is awesome and my jars start to glow

I n my enchanted land, nothing is normal

E xcept for the animals

S afely I wake up in my bed which means it was a dream.

Phoebe Drake-Davis (8)
Newland St John's CE Academy, Hull

The Deadliest Dragon

D eadly as can be

E normous are his teeth, I think I might be his tea

A round the sky, he flies

D odging everything in the skies

L owering himself to the ground

I wish I could send him to the pound

E very step he takes

S haking the earth with the quakes

T hundering is his roar

D o I hear any more?

R aging like a beast

A m I his next feast?

G leaming are his eyes

O h, I wish I was in disguise

N ow I must go before I am eaten by this foe.

Amy Yeomans (9)
Newland St John's CE Academy, Hull

My Dreamland

M ermaids, fairies and unicorns galore
Y ummy sweets all around me

D ragons in caves, mermaids on rocks
R hinoceros eating ice cream
E ating the pavements and grass
A nd meeting dragons as scary as great white sharks
M ermaids underwater, unicorns on rainbows
L lamas eating chips as weird as you eating socks
A nd snakes drinking cola
N aughty elephants squirting water
D ragons roaring louder than thunder.

Imogen Gibson (9)
Newland St John's CE Academy, Hull

Magical World

M any people want to live here

A lways exciting

G et sweets, meet unicorns

I n this world, you see the unimaginable

C areful who you talk to, good or evil?

A ll magical fairies gather here

L ive like a queen

F ly like a butterfly

A goblin might come

I n and scare you

R un from pirates

I n the tunnel, daisies grow

E veryone has joy here

S ee a beautiful sight.

Lois Starkey (9)
Newland St John's CE Academy, Hull

War Of My Dream

W hat has happened to our country?
A fter Adventure Gold Star
R unning quickly to not die

O bviously dangerous
F or goodness sake, there are wars

M y nightmare of all nightmares
Y oung but adventurous

D angerously epic
R andomly picked
E xtra hard work for our sergeant
A ctual blood dripping
M eant to be an easy week.

Jakub Andrzej Wiewiorka (9)
Newland St John's CE Academy, Hull

Otters

O ne day, I dreamt about
T raining otters
T hey are my favourite animal
E ating lots of fish and
R unning around the river

T raining otters is very fun
R aining all day
A t the zoo
I nside, they play
N ever seen such a mess
E very day you clean them out
R eally wish this was not a dream.

Olivia Grace Moore (7)
Newland St John's CE Academy, Hull

Hogwarts

H arry Potter's magical school

O ld castle full of mystery

G oing higher the towers reach the sky

W itches and wizards casting spells

A lbus Dumbledore, the ancient headmaster

R on and Hermione are Harry's best friends

T eachers educating students in magical ways

S lytherin, Hufflepuff, Ravenclaw and Gryffindor are the houses.

Bohan Stephenson-Smith (8)
Newland St John's CE Academy, Hull

How To Write An Acrostic Poem

R ain drops, *drip-drop*, on my shoes
A nd more drops fall in ones and twos
I think of all my friends inside
N *ot me*, I think. *I shall not hide*
S tormy weather makes me run
T o puddles outside, so much fun
O n rainy days, I'll always be
R unning around for all to see
M ud splashes cover me!

Rehema Aliyii Yussuf (9)
Newland St John's CE Academy, Hull

Unicorn Magic

U nder the rainbow, you will see a pot of gold
N ight-time, the rainbow disappears into the clouds
I n the pot of gold, there is a magical coin
C ookies, the yummiest you can taste
O rdering the magic colourful wind
R emove the pot of gold it does not
N o lunch today, we have jobs to do
S parkling potions, pink, blue and purple.

Alesia Maria (8)
Newland St John's CE Academy, Hull

Back To The Dinosaur Era

D inosaurs are scary

I n the Jurassic Era

N obody likes to see dinosaurs

O r they will get eaten

S o they stay away and spy

A s well as seeing dinosaurs, seeing amazing plants

R *oar!* They don't speak

S o it's a scary, exciting and fun dream.

Olivia Laws (9)
Newland St John's CE Academy, Hull

Romans Rule The School

R omans ruling
O ver schools
M aking us their Roman ruler
A lways doing what they can
N ever failing in their plan
S oldiers march here and there

R otten Romans everywhere
U niforms and sandals
L unchtime feasts and light from candles
E ducation Roman style!

Emilia Hayter (7)
Newland St John's CE Academy, Hull

Famous

F ans are happily cheering and shouting my name
A riana Grande is standing right beside me
M able's house is where I am
O utrageous is how I am feeling
U nicorn Popsi gives me a ride home
S at down, had some coffee and ate yummy popcorn!

Bethany Kelechi Iwuchukwu (9)
Newland St John's CE Academy, Hull

Dream Land Adventure

D ream all day about Dream Land
R eally fun
E pic candyfloss
A mazing treats and toys
M agnificent rides

L ights always bright
A nd fun never stops
N ever and, in Dream Land
D isaster never comes.

Millie Grace Norton (8)
Newland St John's CE Academy, Hull

Teachers Strike Back

T rekking around the dark wall
E scaping some escapers
A ll close in and destroy
C lutching their mighty hammers
H eroes deciding to escape
E xcept, "You there!" they cried
"R etreat, they've found us"
S till, just a dream.

Russell Gareth Kneller (9)
Newland St John's CE Academy, Hull

Spell Went Wrong

W and in my hand, a spell I will make

I will change a stick into a snake

Z *ap!* goes my wand

A mazing sight

R ight there in front of me, it wasn't right

D ragons breathing fire

S o scared, I must not be awake.

Dominic Peter Arnold (8)
Newland St John's CE Academy, Hull

Spooky And Scary

Scream-maker
Cold air
Foggy sights
Scary laughs
Frightened screams
Frightening mannequins
Haunting faces
Creaking floorboards
Terrorised children
Terrorising masks
Fake blood
All scary
Traumatised children
Hats and spider shadows
Traumatising shadows.

Freja Tatianah Wensveen (8)
Newland St John's CE Academy, Hull

Evie's Animals

A mazing animals

N ibbles and me

I n a wooden house, I'll be

M e and Mollie learn to roar

A nimals everywhere

L aws are laws

S o don't break the animal laws.

Evie Marie Pamela Lee (7)
Newland St John's CE Academy, Hull

Global Warming

Global warming
Lots of fire
Bikes to hire
Burn the cars
Might be bizarre
But, turn off the light
It will be alright
We have a few more years
To continue with our beautiful circus
What will disappear?
Lots of engineers.

Giuditta Nenye Ugwo (8)
Newland St John's CE Academy, Hull

Unicorn's Pet

U nicorn pet

N ever sad

I am cute

C loud flying

O n top of her

R ed sparkling wings

N ot just red

S weet, beautiful unicorn.

Giulietta Nonye Ugwo (8)
Newland St John's CE Academy, Hull

Volcano

V ery dangerous

O ver the edge, lava overflows

L eaking lava

C racking crust

A sh clouds rising

N ot easy to stop

O vertaking the land.

Connor Walker (8)
Newland St John's CE Academy, Hull

Guitar

G alactic Rick Schuler
U nbelievable music
I mpeccable grades
T iny amps
A mazing books
R eleasing work.

Blake Rose (8)
Newland St John's CE Academy, Hull

Did It Happen?

Gold-lifter
Wind-maker
Defense-maker
Risk-taker
Fire-controller
Pencil-mover
Sport-winner.

Eliza Jane Janus (8)
Newland St John's CE Academy, Hull

Clowns, Superpowers And FBI

C lowns are creepy and scary
L oud clowns making sounds like 'haha'
O w! I can see clowns everywhere
W hat are you doing? Stop killing me!
N ow I'm feeling scared
S top it now, there's blood everywhere!

S uperpowers are amazing stuff
U nderground saving people's lives
P owers are really hard to get
E ven if you don't have superpowers
R eally trying to get superpowers
P roud, be proud of flying
O h my, can you see Spider-Man?
W orking with some superpowers is dangerous
E ven if you go near superpowers
R eally you are going to die
S uperpowers are the best.

F abulous FBI is the beast
B eat the FBI, you get a medal
I think no one can beat the FBI.

Tyler Hartley (9)
Paull Primary School, Paull

Get Lost

G etting lost in the forest, I screamed for someone nice

E ating all the food I can find, I soon get full and happy

T rying to find a way out, I trip over, *ouch!* Then I feel the mud between my fingers

L ooking out from the forest, the sun is brighter than a torch in my eyes

O ver the hill, I see trees waving at me

S o now I have been walking for years, I hear birds sing, I soon dash

T rees lead me to my home safe again.

Emelia Shally (9)
Paull Primary School, Paull

Nature's Dream

I looked around on the forest floor,
Around me, the sun was beaming.
Seas of leaves are falling to the ground,
I thought I was dreaming.

Blossom petals are beautiful
As they fall to the ground.
The rustling leaves
Are a graceful sound.

As the grass danced in the wind...
Splash! I fell in the lake!
Just then I felt hungry,
A cake I must bake.

Birds are singing,
Bees are buzzing,
Some blue-tits fly by,
Grey tits are blushing.

As I stepped on dry leaves
They were crunching
Meanwhile hungry birds
Are gracefully munching

As the wind swooshed by
The blossom snows
A hawk flies by
All the birds froze.

Jasmine Hornsby (9)
Paull Primary School, Paull

Candy Land Superpowers!

One day, I was in bed
And I was dreaming about Candy Land
And powers and it took me to Candy Land
I feel excited and I go to Candy Castle
And it gives me candy powers
I gain the power to fly
And I get a candy costume
I now feel amazed, I also get to eat super candy
I now get to shoot laser candy
Out my eyes, I live in my underground
Candy base with a soft, white bed
I have a sweet-themed house
And a sweet-themed dressing gown
And then I wake up in bed!

Josh Collier (8)
Paull Primary School, Paull

My New Dog

M agnificent magic came to me this day
Y ay! It's Puppy Day! Let's go and play

N ew puppy at 10pm
E verybody dreams we can play
W hile I was on the way to pick up the dog

D ashed into the pet store, I had to get some pet food and a lead, but there was none
O h no! I have two minutes to wait!
G ood, I was on time, time for a cookie, so cute, the best dog ever and it's sitting right there.

Ezmie Rose Butler (8)
Paull Primary School, Paull

Motocross

M iles of riding on the truck with my friend Jack

O ver the jump, I did a whip wash! My bike went

"T ime is over," said Dad, he got in the van and it
went *brum!*

O il is leaking on my bike so I had to fix it

C alling my friends, telling them about my day

"R iding was hard Mum."

O n the sofa, I ate a doughnut

S itting and thinking about my day

S ighing because my bike broke.

Kai Wallace (8)
Paull Primary School, Paull

The Best Teacher Ever

It is just a normal day at Paull Primary School
And our teacher Miss Swatman as she stomped
Bang! Clap! as we were all feeling really happy
Also, Miss Swatman is as lovely as a unicorn

As Miss Swatman is so kind and lovely
I would love to be someone like her
As she is amazing

Miss Swatman is the best teacher ever
Also when I'm old I would like to be a teacher
And she teaches Class Two!

Scarlet Faulkner (8)
Paull Primary School, Paull

My Dream

I am a footballer just about to enter Anfield
They started the game
The whistle is as loud as a lion
Thirty minutes into the game, I score
Whoop! The snow dances in the wind

Someone gets a red card
I hope it's not me... *Phew!*
I run down the pitch
I score again and again
The crowd goes wild
The game ends.

Drew Hicks (7)
Paull Primary School, Paull

Football Dream!

In my dream
It includes a ball
I love to play sports
And make people fall

I play number six
To shoot then score
If I keep doing this
I would never be poor

Watching people shoot
With a goalie shouting, "I see!"
I like to say unlucky
But people just ignore me

This is my dream
I hope it comes true
It better work for me
Then work for you too!

Kacey Doney (9)
Paull Primary School, Paull

Fairies

F airies have wands
A tooth fairy takes teeth and gives money
I love fairies with their wings
R are fairies are green fairies in the beautiful woods
I ce fairies make snow and snowflakes
E verybody loves fairies even boys
S un fairies make sunshine and make it nice and
warm.

Holly Emma Witty (8)
Paull Primary School, Paull

Headmaster

H appy day for a headmaster
E at a lot at dinner time
A bout when children aren't enough
D etention for children
M aster of the school
A nd nice to kids
S illy as a goose
T ight belt every time
E ach teacher is a server
R eally tall.

Ethan Shane Gravill (9)
Paull Primary School, Paull

Detective

D ancing around all night
E very case in the city
T he criminal's running away
E verything but crime
C risis cases in mountains
T en o'clock shifts
I vy and trees to camouflage in
V enom with guns
E ating food while searching.

Harry York (8)
Paull Primary School, Paull

My Dream Teacher

T eaching is my future

E ngaging my children to work

A nd the children's best subject is maths

C all their parents, they have been naughty

H abitat is not what they're learning

E ngaging their children to read

R eading they did, for ten minutes

Lillie-Maya Bentley (8)

Paull Primary School, Paull

Army Man

A s I go out to war, I feel frightened
R iding in the jeep, getting closer to the battlefields
M oving closer, seeing the bombs getting dropped
Y oung soldier running

M oving fast, shooting the enemy
A sking when it will end
N agging for food.

Ethan Zevan Butler (8)
Paull Primary School, Paull

Unicorn

U nique animals around the world

N ew animals appearing every day

I see a unicorn dancing and prancing

C andy fell from the sky

O ne of the unicorns saw me, I was trying to stroke him and

R an as fast as a cheetah

N ow I can't find him.

Evie Kirkwood (8)
Paull Primary School, Paull

Fairies

F airies always know how to fly
A fairy has always got to have fun
I love having friends every day
R eally funny fairies coming to play
I really like having friends
E very fairy knows how to make friends
S illy, laughing fairies.

Eve Alexandra Valentine (7)
Paull Primary School, Paull

Nitro

N itro Circus pro MX rider, better than Travis Pastrana

I ntroduction by Ben Warrington backflipping, jumps in front of thousands of people

T ravis is bad and Ben is better

R ight at Mickey Field practising whips

O nly one Ben Warrington.

Ben Warrington (9)

Paull Primary School, Paull

Tooth Fairy

The Tooth Fairy gave me three pounds.
Everybody loses their baby teeth
And everybody gets gold coins.
The Tooth Fairy has a purple sparkly dress,
She is so small.
Her wings are so sparkly and they help her fly.
Look how beautiful the Tooth Fairy is.

Sophia Jazmine Gwynne (8)
Paull Primary School, Paull

Me And My Career

I went to the Hollywood filming place
I met Elton John, my teacher is Miss Swatman
I am a fan of Good Morning
Tomorrow I might go to my mum's

I liked the reaction of Queen
Then, I walked home
I hated Avengers Endgame.

Carter Grantam (8)
Paull Primary School, Paull

The Potion

I was going to find a potion
In the dark, scary forest
Me, wearing a black hoodie, green coat and some white gloves
And hunting like a dumb dog

Two wolves came running, running, running
Me covering my face like a scaredy-cat
They sat down on the spot and said, "Need help, Ma'am?"
I stood in shock like a statue
I answered back with a simple, "Yes."

I told them I needed to find a potion
So they started helping me
We looked around in the forest
No luck, no potion

One of the wolves started acting strange
His eyes were a nightmare
He kept looking at something that I was trying to find
It was the potion

I grabbed the potion as fast as I could
The crazy wolf roared and hissed like a lion

I jumped on the other wolf's back and told her to get
us out of here
The wolf ran as fast as she could, but the psychopath
was even faster

It bit my leg
I screamed like I was a baby
I hit his face with my other foot and he fell in a deep,
deep hole
We escaped the forest
I said thank you to the wolf and left
I healed and put a bandage on my bitten foot

I went outside my lovely garden
Trying to find the perfect spot
I put the liquid of the potion on the spot
And waited for the sunflower to grow...

Maria Tudose (10)
Queens Road Academy, Barnsley

The Horrible Nightmares

N othing has been stranger than this day
I woke up and I looked through the window
"G uys, where are you?" a voice said
"H ere!" another voice screamed
T *rot, trot,* a horse was in my room
"M y horse!" a cowboy shouted
A massive spaceship crashed into my house
"R oar!" a monster roared
"E nd of the world!" my brother yelled
S o I jumped out of my window

"A rgh!" I cried and the monster repeated
"R oar!" and again and again and again
E *nd of the world,* I thought

"B radley," I heard my mother say
A nd I woke up. "It was just a horrible
D ream," I said.

Frank Millkowski (10)
Queens Road Academy, Barnsley

Disneyland Dream

Once there was a young child who had many
wonderful dreams
That she wanted to achieve, but they never ever came
true
She began to lose hope
Therefore, her great goals in future life would be
ruined!
The problem with her dreams never becoming true
Was that she had totally lost hope!
The next morning, she woke up with happiness
And, unbelievably, more hope
She gently opened her eyes to reveal
That she was in her favourite place: Disneyland!
Which proves that dreams can come true but
You must believe in yourself to follow your destiny!

Hannah Rose Johnson (10)
Queens Road Academy, Barnsley

A Dream Of A Creature

Lying in my bed
I could not go to sleep
Where would we go?
What creature would we meet?

Walking down the lane
Walking down the street
What magical creature
Will I meet?

Out of the corner of my eye
I saw a massive flash
A massive burst of rubbish
Also known as trash
Just pushed past really fast

As I walked into the fire
I saw a whole lot more
Rainbow fairies
And even a unicorn

I never want to go away
Because this is what I like
Swim with dolphins and have fun
And that is alright.

Lola Frances Sanderson (10)
Ravenfield Primary School, Ravenfield

Fashionista

A party, exciting! But oh, what to wear?
The clothes, the make-up, what to do with my hair?
A spray tan, fake nails and false lashes to put on
Jewellery from Tiffany and belt, Louis Vuitton
Next to the salon to do my hair
Blonde, straight and curls to flair
The make-up is MAC the outfits all Gucci
The shoes and the handbag are true Prada beauties
Dressed in designer from head to toe
The limo arrives and we're ready to go.

Romanie Alice Easthope (10)
Ravenfield Primary School, Ravenfield

What A Good Dream

I went to bed once I had a good sleep
In the night, I heard my cat weep
He wanted a submarine
So I built him one that was clean
We went underwater
And had some glee
We saw a shark
He had a good bark
There was a colony of fish
They made a big wish
The fuel ran out
So we swam out
We found a rocket in my back pocket
We flew away to Jupiter and Spain
Then I woke to the sound of rain.

Alex Watson (10)
Ravenfield Primary School, Ravenfield

The Storm

I'm in my house lifting three hundred kilograms weight
Then somebody lures you from the dark shadow and
the storm
In fact, two people come from the dark shadow!
They were both clowns, one has a picklock and one has
a toy gun

Then, I heard a noise and the noise went *bang!*
As the storm raged on, the rain has somehow turned
into Fanta
I looked behind my back and I saw Charizard and
Pikachu
When Pikachu fired a bolt of lightning out of his hand, I
burped weirdly

When I saw the doorknob turning, I got even more
scared
I thought my ears are broken because of Charizard's
roar
I quickly phoned the police
Nevermind because I'm back in bed.

George Sainsbury (8)
Saltburn Primary School, Saltburn-By-The-Sea

The Battle

Daleks zooming across the sky like planes
Crashing in my bunker, whooshing spaceships up
above
The emperor Dalek blabbering commands from the
littered garden

Finally, I hear peace, but again, "Exterminate!"
The battle starts, a Dalek breaks into my bunker
I frantically run for the teleporter, *zap!*
I teleport to Africa. Oh no! The Daleks followed me

Battle in Africa, what a sight!
What a fight!
Zap! No! I got shot and I'm dead...

Eddie Dolphin (8)
Saltburn Primary School, Saltburn-By-The-Sea

Alex The DJ

When I woke up in my bedroom
I had a robot arm and some DJ stuff
And I thought I was a DJ
It was cool
I wore my red trainers
And went outside, running to my own concert
And I had lots of fun with my fans
My fans were really cool
I didn't even know I had fans
But I stopped and it was my bedtime
So I went back home and snored in my bed
Next morning, I woke up and I had breakfast
And asked my mum to let me go out to party
So that's what I did.

Alex Grant (8)
Saltburn Primary School, Saltburn-By-The-Sea

The Unnamed Nightmare

I walk and walk until an insect attacks
My cat screams, "No!"
It is like a house being exposed
I run and run until I see a battle of Pokémon

They turn and attack, I say, "Help me!"
I still run for the opposite way
I get caught, this is bad
The giant drips all around the place

Lightning hits everything. *Bang!* It hits a pig
The mouse was hit and said, "Tik!"
A giant laughs and laughs as well
All is well!

Henry James Robinson (8)
Saltburn Primary School, Saltburn-By-The-Sea

Evil Sprout Spiders

I am flying in the air in such a fright
I don't know what to do
All I can see is lots of light
The sun's in my eyes
And I have been told too many lies

Slurp went the evil sprout spiders
My heart was bouncing
I was so scared
I was making my own words like, "Wipltyiders."

Finally, I'm back home
And I'm happy as a child on Christmas Day
Everybody's happy to see me
So at least I'm not alone.

Alfie Robert Gregory (8)
Saltburn Primary School, Saltburn-By-The-Sea

The Crystal Kingdom

Once upon a time when the sun was out
A beautiful unicorn was going to have a baby girl
And when she had the baby
Silver, the mum unicorn, named the baby unicorn
Madiz

One day, two naughty fairies took the baby's horn
And her mum had to go on a magical adventure

On the way, they have to go to the city
And they made friends with all the cats
When they found the horn
They taught the fairies to be good.

Ellie Cochrane (7)
Saltburn Primary School, Saltburn-By-The-Sea

My Lovely Dream

I live in my lovely, pretty, fluffy, unicorn, rainbow home
It's big inside and colourful
With the soft, rainbow, unicorn furniture
And fluffy on the outside
It is shaped like a horn

The hair is very, very pretty and shiny
The ears are very, very pointy
And the windows are unicorn shape
At the top is gold and very, very shiny
The flowers in the bushes with rainbow petals
That glisten in the sun.

Evie Marie Preston (7)
Saltburn Primary School, Saltburn-By-The-Sea

Wizard Land

W izard practising at a castle
I n a castle, wizards live
Z ooming through the air
A wizard conjures up some magic
R oars from underneath the castle, there
D eep down in the basement, there's a snake

L eaping dragons
A mazing potions
N agging witches
D angerous spells.

Samuel Robson (8)
Saltburn Primary School, Saltburn-By-The-Sea

Toy World

D riving along the track in my Hot Wheels car as fast as the wind

R uling the country in my house of Lego

E very evil man who wants to rule me and Wu will stop

A n apple flies past and a banana zooms across the sky

M aster Wu helps me save the world

S inging like a hummingbird, Lego men march past.

Ollie Dolphin (8)
Saltburn Primary School, Saltburn-By-The-Sea

Chocolate Monkey And The Enchanted Castle

In the beautiful sky lived a chocolate monkey
He loves to fly over candyfloss and clouds
One day, he was flying over candyfloss clouds
When he got right above the clouds, he saw a castle
He wasn't sure what was in it, so he went to check it out
When he got inside, he saw a giant
The giant didn't like the chocolate monkey
So the giant ate him.

Izak Rees (8)
Saltburn Primary School, Saltburn-By-The-Sea

Devil To Candyfloss

Devil in the colossal arena
Noise among the crowd
Blood-red coloured devils fighting
The crowd is shouting for joy
And shouting in excitement

The devils fight for the prize of candyfloss
The devils have shields magical and mysterious
The strangest thing
A child devil won the delicious candyfloss!

Talay Dechbamrung (8)
Saltburn Primary School, Saltburn-By-The-Sea

The Big Discovery

Far, far away there were two boys
Named Jacob and Tommy
Tommy's heart flies out like an eagle
I ran to reach it
But I ran into a big time machine
What was that?
It was a time machine!

I went into the time machine
Whoosh I opened the door
And it was Chocolate World...

Jacob Williamson (7)
Saltburn Primary School, Saltburn-By-The-Sea

My Dream

D evils fighting goblins
R ed devils on candy mountains
E very knight driving planes to escape
A gents running to their base to hide
M any goblins trying to take out planes
S o many people fighting and hiding.

Oscar William Gill (8)
Saltburn Primary School, Saltburn-By-The-Sea

Picachu And The Pot Of Gold

D ancing underneath a rainbow
R aichu is with me
E ating candy while we start to fall asleep
A nd we see a pot of gold
M y friend Raichu takes the gold
S o now we are rich.

Lorraine Crown (8)
Saltburn Primary School, Saltburn-By-The-Sea

Nightmare

N ight approaches and my nightmares escape

I n my dreams came a scary face

G lory spreads on the black ground

"H elp! Help!" I was shouting out loud

"T he spirits of hell are running after me!"

M y legs were running fast, don't you see?

A nd my heart was intensely beating

R apidly, their scars were bleeding

E ventually, I found out I was safe in my bed!

Hana Qaisar (9)
Southroyd Primary School, Pudsey

Once Upon A Dream I Was A Great Footballer

Once upon a dream
I was a footballer, the best footballer on the team
With a blue kit and a Tottenham sign
I was a footballer, the best footballer on the team
With every match, the team was proud of me
I was a footballer, the best footballer on the team
We were so happy
I scored four goals, finals, here we come!

As we went to our captain's house to celebrate
We saw our opponents practising with everything they had
I was worried, the most worried footballer on the team

It was the day of the big match
I was scared and missed twenty-five goals
I was the worst, the worst footballer on the team
With the final score being six-nil, everybody was angry with me
I was embarrassed, the most embarrassed footballer on the team

As we went to our captain's house
They wanted me gone
I was devastated, the most devastated footballer on
the team

In the next game, we suddenly got a penalty
I was taking it, as I stepped up
I shot it and it hit the crossbar
I fell to my knees with my hand over my mouth
All of a sudden, the ball descended and went past the
line
It was a goal
I was relieved and, with ninety minutes gone
The final score was one-nil
My teammates ran over and congratulated me
I was ecstatic, the most ecstatic footballer on the team

Although we were out of the tournament
I was happy that I was back to my normal self
I was the best, the best footballer on the team.

Harry Fletcher (8)
Southroyd Primary School, Pudsey

Unicorns And Fairies Dance In My Head

As I lay in bed, ready to dream
I dream of unicorns and much more
I remember a nature fairy
Whose favourite colour was green
As unicorns and fairies dance in my head
I hugged them as if they were my favourite ted
As I lie down on my big, fluffy bed
And then I'm in a dream, chocolate in sight
As I put on my nightlight
And then, I say,
"Goodnight unicorns and fairies, we had a good day."

Lily Mai Fitzpatrick (9)
Sunnyfields Primary School, Scawthorpe

Underwater Paradise

I dreamed a dream last night
As I lay in my comfy bed
The large warm sun made the ocean bright
And the long, green kelp bashed against my head

I dived between foamy, turquoise water with a whoosh
I swam past enchanting coves
And, because I was so loud, the tropical fish told me to hush
The colourful coral seemed to be their homes

I swam with a herd of bottle-nosed dolphins
I danced with vivid, red crabs as they scattered
I avoided salty sharks who would find me delish
"This is a wonderful dream," I muttered
(So the fish don't tell me to hush again)
(The amount of time they've done that is around ten!)

I felt the soft sand and liquid fluid water
I even borrowed a pristine, smooth pearl from a clam's daughter
As I woke up I was missing my dream
And to continue I turned over in my pillow that smelled of whipped cream!

Lucy White (10)
The Parks Academy, Orchard Park Estate

My Dream

I had a dream in bed last night
Of places most bizarre
My house was full of sweets
People were eating the treats
The chocolate trees are dancing in the breeze
They are very tall
Unicorns prance
While the trees and I danced

Stars twinkle playfully
When the wooden planks laugh as I told them a joke
I ran past all the chocolate trees
All my friends are running around with feathered,
buzzing bees

My awesome dream is great
Especially when I'm playing with
My kind, friendly, caring mates
I have had a fabulous day
We all love to play
We pretend to fly and go *whoosh* in the sky!

Kacey-Leigh R (10)
The Parks Academy, Orchard Park Estate

Once Upon A Dream

I had a dream in bed last night
Which started with a bright light
But out of it came things I've never seen!
Like sugar rain and candy canes
Things I love to eat

As I entered through the yawning gate
I heard the sound of angels
The birds tweeting in tune
Trees swaying
I said, "What lovely music is this?"

Along with this, the smell of freshly baked bread
Ran up my nose, bringing me back to life
Bang! The candy popping, making my taste buds smile

I walked through the fields of jelly beans
And over fondant hills
But then the dream just ended
With my pillow...

Daniel Etornam Tsenuokpor (10)
The Parks Academy, Orchard Park Estate

The Fireworks And Stars

On bonfire night, I had a fright
Fireworks went *fizz, pop, bang*
And danced with the stars
The jelly bears upon the ground
Cheering the fireworks on

The shooting stars and the lightning scars
What weird things to see
I jumped up on a fluffy cloud
I flew in the sky like a bird
I danced upon with the fireworks
Fizzing as you can see

I saw the colours of the rainbows
Smiling at me trying to say bye
I went home and peered out the window
To the colourful sky waving goodbye

Once again, the curtains closed
I woke to find my sister smiling at me.

Emelia G (10)
The Parks Academy, Orchard Park Estate

I Dreamed A Dream Of Randomness

I dreamed a dream on my couch last night
And it was most bizarre
Of cakes and buns and chocolate biscuits
Dancing beneath the golden stars

My pen clicks as I put the lid on
I see a radiator and it automatically turns on
My friend goes in red
When we move the name, it goes *flick!*

I see a small lovely factory
That smells of freshly baked bread
I see a chip shop that is blue

The red door opens for school
Everyone runs inside
The red rock-solid door
Is as hard as a metal whiteboard.

Courtney G (10)
The Parks Academy, Orchard Park Estate

My Dream

I dreamed a dream in bed last night
Of places so brilliant
Of bellowing lightning
Of crispy, brown leaves
And candy trees

Of flowers like jelly beans
And candy, green trees
Of waterfalls quite high
Bigger than you can fly

Of singing rocks
When you talk
Dogs that danced and pranced
And centipedes that danced

There are neon centipedes with a song
And crocodiles that yell, "Bang!"
I drove into a pea-green bush
With a *whoosh*
What a great dream.

Keegan Markham (10)
The Parks Academy, Orchard Park Estate

My Dreams

Whether I was soaring high
Meeting royalty
Watching flowers dance in the breeze
Or learning fun wizardry

Tweet! Tweet! Tweet!
Bluebirds sang
Monkeys climbed
Then crash with a bang

A rosy scent as
A unicorn flew
Something to me
Felt so new

Climb in a soft silky bed
Woke up and found
I sleep-walked to a river
About to drown!

Amari Ja Leigh Williamson (10)
The Parks Academy, Orchard Park Estate

What Will Your Dream Be?

I n your crazy world, have you ever dreamed to be

M agical and marvellous, oh what about a tree?

A superhero searching and zooming through the skies

G lamorous and wonderful, oh could you be

I magination, oh imagination, oh what will your dream be?

N ever-ending stories of pirates and heroes

A dog named Tom or a cat called Spot

T he tables to dance and the chairs to sing

I n your mighty dream, what would it be?

O range, red and purple colours around

N ever hesitate and reach for your dreams!

Victoria Glod (11)
Townfield Primary School, Doncaster

Sweet Dreams Ava

"S weet dreams," Ava's Mum always says
W hen I close my eyes, I count the sheep
E leven, twelve, thirteen slowly fade away
E lves and fairies came to play
T ogether, we have so much fun

D ifferent animals all around
R eindeer, unicorns wear a crown
E erie castles stand up tall
A nd make the cottages seem so small
M any adventures we will have
S o much wonder in this land

"A va, it's time to get up."
V ery slowly, my eyes start to open
A lovely start to a brand new day.

Ava Rose Robinson (9)
West Road Primary School, Moorends

Rainbow Badge

I've often heard my mum talk about the rainbow bridge
But didn't know what it was
She'd sit and cry at Facebook and wouldn't tell me why
Then one day, Sasha went away
While I was at school and
When my mum told me where she'd gone, I cried
I'd like to see this rainbow bridge
And see our Sasha again and say goodbye
My mum always said, "Wish!"
So I wish it would come true
But all I got from Mum is, "One day!"

Sophie Newham (9)
West Road Primary School, Moorends

YOUNG WRITERS INFORMATION

We hope you have enjoyed reading this book – and that you will continue to in the coming years.

If you're a young writer who enjoys reading and creative writing, or the parent of an enthusiastic poet or story writer, do visit our website **www.youngwriters.co.uk**. Here you will find free competitions, workshops and games, as well as recommended reads, a poetry glossary and our blog.

If you would like to order further copies of this book, or any of our other titles, then please give us a call or visit **www.youngwriters.co.uk**.

Young Writers
Remus House
Coltsfoot Drive
Peterborough
PE2 9BF
(01733) 890066
info@youngwriters.co.uk